I'm special

WAYLAND

Your Feelings

I'm bored	I'm shy
I'm lonely	I'm happy
I'm worried	I'm special
It's not fair	I feel bullied

find Wayland on the Internet at http://www.wayland.co.uk

First published in 1999 by
Wayland Publishers Ltd
61 Western Road, Hove
East Sussex BN3 1JD, England

✓ Find out about how this book is relevant to
the National Literacy Strategy on page 31.

Series editor: Alex Woolf
Designer: Jean Wheeler
Consultant: Nick Tapp, Deputy Chief Executive, East Sussex
Disability Association

British Library Cataloguing in Publication Data
Green, Jen, 1955-
I'm special. - (Your feelings)
1. Handicapped - Juvenile literature
I. Title
362.4

ISBN 0-7502-2357-X

Typeset by Jean Wheeler
Printed and bound in Italy by G. Canale & C.S.p.A., Turin

I'm special

Written by Jen Green

Illustrated by Mike Gordon

WAYLAND

My name is Sarah. You could say I'm special. My legs don't work properly, so I use a wheelchair to get about.

I love music, and play the recorder in our school orchestra.

I love animals,
especially our cat
and dog.

My best friend Jo is also special. She's a whizz at maths and science.

She can't see well, but her calculator speaks to her out loud.

Our friend Ben is special too. He's the champion swimmer in our class.

Ben can't hear much. He has a hearing aid.

He watches people's lips to find out what they are saying.

When people stare or point at me
as I go by, I feel shy.

Sometimes I think they are scared because I am special, not quite the same as them.

When people talk to Jo as if she's stupid, she feels upset.

She can't see well, but she's just as quick as them.

When other kids tease Ben behind his back so he can't hear them, he feels angry.

But he talks in signs to his friend Jeff instead.

When my brother leaves me out of games like football, I feel sad.

Last week when I played with the others, I scored a goal!

When grown-ups ignore me and talk to Mum as if I wasn't there, I feel cross.

'Ask me!
I can speak
for myself,
you know!'

When buildings have so many stairs I can't go in, I feel left out.

But the new sports centre has lifts and ramps, and we have great fun there.

Some grown-ups I know
are special too. They all
seem very busy.

Hannah's mum has a wheelchair ...

and drives a fast, shiny car.

Mrs Mills, from our street,
is the boss of a big office.

Mr Black is the head teacher at our school.

When grown-ups fuss and try to help with something I can do, I feel embarrassed.

Let me chop this up for you.

26

It's OK when children who are special take longer to do something, or do it in a different way.

Often I like to be treated just the same as everyone else.

Everyone finds some things hard and some things easy.

Everyone is different and special, just like me.

Notes for parents and teachers

This book provides an introduction to the subject of disability for young children. Parents or teachers who have read the book with children, either individually or in groups, may find it useful to stop and discuss issues as they come up.

Ask children to name all the different kinds of disability they can think of. Talk about different disabilities, including mental disabilities. Encourage children to imagine what it is like to be disabled by making their way from the blackboard to their desk blindfold, or by trying to understand the lesson while covering their ears. Ask children to do a survey of their home, classroom or the whole school, making a list of the difficulties that would be encountered by a child in a wheelchair. (Are there many stairs? Are pegs, lockers and other facilities at the right height? Are toilets accessible?) Talk about ways in which buildings can be changed to make things easier for disabled people.

This book describes a number of attitudes and reactions that people with disabilities encounter frequently. Common reactions include staring, ignoring disabled people, providing help before asking if any is needed, and making assumptions or patronising comments. Explain that many disabled people feel their biggest disadvantage is other people's attitudes towards them. Encourage the children to act out real or imaginary encounters between disabled and able-bodied children. Then suggest that children exchange roles. How would they feel if they were treated as disabled people often are? How would they resolve the situation? Other children can comment on whether the scenes acted out were realistic or not.

Alternatively, children may like to write list poems that explore the feelings of people with disabilities:

When I can't see the new film at the cinema because there are too many stairs, I feel left out.

When you shout at me as if I'm stupid, I feel hurt and angry.

Explore the fact that sometimes people try to insult others by using words that describe people with various disabilities. Explain that name-calling is cruel and hurtful, like racism. Children may decide that name-calling is not acceptable, and that they will challenge it. Parents can help by exploring their own attitudes to disability, and realizing that their attitudes influence their children.

Use this book for teaching literacy

This book can help you in the literacy hour in the following ways:

- ✓ Children can write simple stories linked to personal experience using the language of the text in this book as a model for their own writing. (Year 1, Term 3: Non-fiction writing composition)

- ✓ Children can look through the book and try to locate verbs with past and present tense endings. (Year 1, Term 3: Word recognition, graphic knowledge and spelling)

- ✓ Use of speech bubbles and enlarged print shows different ways of presenting texts. (Year 2, Term 2: Sentence construction and punctuation)

Books to read

Something Else written by Wendy Lohse, illustrated by Leigh Murrell (Hodder and Stoughton, 1989). When Bronwyn arrives for her first day at school, Buster taunts her because she has no legs. But Bronwyn is quietly confident. Gradually Buster and the others find out all the things that Bronwyn can do, and what her special 'something else' is.

Peter Gets a Hearing Aid by Nigel Snell (Hamish Hamilton, 1979). When Peter's parents discover their son can't hear properly, they take Peter to the ear doctor to be fitted with a hearing aid. Now he can hear everyone much better – everyone except his pet tortoise, that is.

I Use a Wheelchair written by Althea, illustrated by John Davey (Dinosaur Publications, 1983). A girl in a wheelchair tells her own story, and explains that other people's attitudes sometimes make her upset and angry. 'Just because I use a wheelchair, doesn't mean I am stupid or silly.'

Christopher's Story by Elizabeth Reuter (Century Hutchinson, 1989). Five-year-old Christopher is always feeling tired. When the doctors find out he has leukaemia, it takes all Christopher's strength and determination to get better.